Lao-Tzu's Tao and Wu Wei

Lao-Tzu's Tao and Wu Wei

by Lao-Tzu

Translated by Dwight Goddard and Henri Borel

Start Publishing PD LLC
Copyright © 2024 by Start Publishing PD LLC

All rights reserved, including the right to reproduce this book or portions thereof in any form whatsoever.

Start Publishing PD is a registered trademark of Start Publishing PD LLC
Manufactured in the United States of America

Cover art: Shutterstock/Taisiya Kozorez

Cover design: Jennifer Do

10 9 8 7 6 5 4 3 2 1

ISBN 979-8-8809-0711-3

Preface

I love Laotzu! That is the reason I offer another interpretative translation, and try to print and bind it attractively. I want you to appreciate this wise and kindly old man, and come to love him. He was perhaps the first of scholars (6th century B.C.) to have a vision of spiritual reality, and he tried so hard to explain it to others, only, in the end, to wander away into the Great Unknown in pathetic discouragement. Everything was against him; his friends misunderstood him; others made fun of him.

Even the written characters which he must use to preserve his thought conspired against him. They were only five thousand in all, and were ill adapted to express mystical and abstract ideas. When these characters are translated accurately, the translation is necessarily awkward and obscure. Sinologues have unintentionally done him an injustice by their very scholarship. I have tried to peer through the clumsy characters into his heart and prayed that love for him would make me wise to understand aright.

I hate scholarship that would deny his existence, or arrogant erudition that says patronizingly, "Oh, yes, there doubtless was some one who wrote some of the characteristic sonnets, but most of them are an accumulation through the centuries of verses that have similar structure, and all have been changed and amended until it is better to call the book a collection of aphorisms."

Shame on scholarship when, sharing the visions of the illuminati, they deride them!

There are three great facts in China to-day that vouch for Lao-tzu. First, the presence of Taoism,--which was suggested by his teachings, not founded upon them. This is explained by the inability of the scholars, who immediately followed him to understand and appreciate the spirituality of his teachings. Second, Confucian dislike for Lao-tzian ideas, which is explained by their opposition to Confucian ethics. Third, and the greatest fact of all, is the characteristic traits of Chinese nature, namely, passivity, submissiveness and moral concern, all of which find an adequate cause and source in the teachings of Lao-tzu.

An interesting fact in regard to the thought of Lao-tzu is this. Although for two thousand years he has been misunderstood and derided, to-day the very best of scientific and philosophic thought, which gathers about what is known as Vitalism, is in full accord with Lao-tzu's idea of the Tao. Every reference that is made to-day to a Cosmic Urge, Vital Impulse, and Creative Principle can be said of the Tao. Everything that can be said of Plato's Ideas and Forms and of Cosmic Love as being the creative expression of God can be said of the Tao. When Christian scholars came to translate the Logos of St. John, they were satisfied to use the word "Tao."

It is true that Lao-tzu's conception of the Tao was limited to a conception of a universal, creative principle. He apparently had no conception of personality, which the Christians ascribe to God, in connection with it, but he ascribed so much of wisdom and benevolence to it that his conception fell little short of personality. To Lao-tzu, the Tao is the universal and eternal principle which forms and conditions everything; it is that intangible cosmic influence which harmonizes all things and brings them to fruition; it is the norm and standard of truth and morality. Lao-tzu did more than entertain an intelligent opinion of Tao as a creative principle; he had a devout and religious sentiment towards it: "He loved the Tao as a son cherishes and reveres his mother."

There are three key words in the thought of Lao-tzu: Tao, Teh, and Wu Wei. They are all difficult to translate. The simple meaning of Tao is "way," but it also has a wide variety of other meanings Dr. Paul Carus translates it, "Reason," but apologizes for so doing. If forced to offer a translation we would suggest Creative Principle, but much prefer to leave it untranslated.

The character, "Teh," is usually translated "virtue." This is correct as a mere translation of the, character, but is in, no sense adequate to the content of the thought in Lao-tzu's mind. To him, Teh meant precisely what is meant in the account of the healing of the woman who touched the hem of Jesus' robe: "Jesus was conscious that virtue had passed from him." Teh includes the meaning of vitality, of virility, of beauty and the harmony that we think of as that part of life that is abounding and joyous. The third word is the negative expression, "Wu Wei." Translated, this means "not acting," or "non-assertion." When Lao-tzu urges men to "wu wei," he is not urging them to laziness or asceticism. He means that all men are to cherish that wise humility and diffidence and selflessness which comes from a consciousness that the Tao is infinitely wise and good, and that the part of human wisdom is to hold one's self in such a restrained and receptive manner that the Tao may find one a suitable and conforming channel for its purpose. The title of Lao-tzu's book, Tao Teh King, is carelessly translated, The Way of Virtue

Classic, or The Way and Virtue Classic. This is very inadequate. The Vitality of the Tao is very much better.

Most commentators think that Lao-tzu's teachings fit in especially well with Buddhist philosophy This conclusion is arrived at by the common interpretation of wu wei as submission that will logically end in absorption of the spirit in Tao as Nirvana. This understanding of wu wei, which Henri Borel shares in a measure, is, we believe, incorrect, inasmuch as Lao-tzu consistently teaches a finding of life rather than a losing of it. Lao-tzu's conception of Tao as the underived Source of all things, finding expression through spiritual Teh in universal creative activity, is very close to Plato's doctrine of the good as the One ineffable Source of all things, whose Ideas and Forms of Goodness, Truth and Beauty radiated outward as spiritual logos in creative activity through Spirit, Soul and Nature to the farthest confines of matter.

While it is true that Lao-tzu's teachings would find little in common with the Old Testament anthropomorphic autocracy, and would find almost nothing in common with the modern Ritschlean system of ethical idealism which has for its basis a naturalistic evolution of human society by means of philanthropy, laws, cultural civilizations, and human governments backed by force of arms, nevertheless his teachings are entirely in harmony with that Christian philosophy of the Logos, which is a heritage from the Greeks, through Plato, Philo, St. Paul, Plotinus, and Augustine, and which is the basis of the mystical faith of the Christian saints of all ages. While Lao-tzu would find little in common with the busy, impertinent activities of so-called Christian statesman building by statecraft and war, he would find much in common with Apostolic Christianity which held itself aloof from current politics and refused to enter the army, content to live simply, quietly, full of faith and humble benevolence.

And most of all would he find himself in sympathy with the teacher of Nazareth. At almost every Sonnet, one thinks of some corresponding expression of Jesus, who had a very similar conception of God, but who recognized in Him that personal element of Love which made God not only Creative Principle but Heavenly Father.

Lao-tzu's vision of the virile harmony, goodness, and Spirituality of the Tao was what Jesus saw as the Fatherhood of God, self-expressing his love-nature endlessly in all creative effort, and, through universal intuition, endlessly drawing his creation back to himself in grateful and humble affection. Lao-tzu saw in a glass darkly what Jesus saw face to face in all his glory, the Divine Tao, God as creative and redemptive Love.

As you read these verses, forget the words and phrases, poor material and poor workmanship at best, look through them for the soul of Lao-tzu. It is there revealed, but so imperfectly that it is only an apparition of a soul. But if by it, vague as it is, you come to love Lao-tzu, you will catch beyond him fleeting glimpses of the splendid visions that so possessed his soul, visions of Infinite Goodness, Humility and Beauty radiating from the Heart of creation.

Dwight Goddard

All We Know about Lao-Tzu

SZE MA-CH'IEN (136-85 B.C.) wrote that Lao-tzu was born of the Li family of Ch'u-jen Village, Li County, Wu Province, Ch'u State. His proper name was Err, his official name was Poh-yang, his posthumous title was Yueh-tan. He held the position of custodian of the secret archives of the State of Cheu.

Confucius went to Cheu to consult Lao-tzu about certain ceremonials; Laotzu told him: "The bones of these sages, concerning whom you inquire, have long since decayed, only their teachings remain. If a superior man is understood by his age, he rises to honor, but not being understood, his name is like a vagrant seed blown about by the wind. I have heard it said that a good merchant conceals his treasures, as though his warehouses were empty. The sage of highest worth assumes a countenance and outward mien as though he were stupid. Put aside your haughty airs, your many needs, affected robes and exaggerated importance. These add no real value to your person. That is my advice to you, and it is all I have to offer."

Confucius departed and when he later described to his students his visit to Lao-tzu, he said: "I understand about the habits of birds, how they can fly; how fish can swim; and animals run. For the running we can make snares, for the swimming we can make nets, for the flying we can make arrows. But for the dragon, I cannot know how he ascends on the winds and clouds to heaven. I have just seen Lao-tzu. Can it be said, he is as difficult to understand as the dragon? He teaches the vitality of Tao. His doctrine appears to lead one to aspire after self-effacement and obscurity."

Lao-tzu lived in Cheu for a long time; he prophesied the decay of that state and in consequence was obliged to depart, and went to the frontier. The officer at the border post was Yin-hi, who said to Lao-tzu, "If you are going to leave us, will you not write a book by which we may remember you?" Thereupon Lao-tzu wrote a book of sonnets in two parts, comprising in all about five thousand characters. In this book he discussed his conception of the Vitality of the Tao. He left this book with the soldier, and departed, no one knows whither.

1

The Tao that can be understood cannot be the primal, or cosmic, Tao, just as an idea that can be expressed in words cannot be the infinite idea.

And yet this ineffable Tao was the source of all spirit and matter, and being expressed was the mother of all created things.

Therefore not to desire the things of sense is to know the freedom of spirituality; and to desire is to learn the limitation of matter. These two things spirit and matter, so different in nature, have the same origin. This unity of origin is the mystery of mysteries, but it is the gateway to spirituality.

2

When every one recognizes beauty to be only a masquerade, then it is simply ugliness. In the same way goodness, if it is not sincere, is not goodness. So existence and non-existence are incompatible. The difficult and easy are mutually opposites. Just as the long and the short, the high and the low, the loud and soft, the before and the behind, are all opposites and each reveals the other.

Therefore the wise man is not conspicuous in his affairs or given to much talking. Though troubles arise he is not irritated. He produces but does not own; he acts but claims no merit; he builds but does not dwell therein; and because he does not dwell therein he never departs.

3

Neglecting to praise the worthy deters people from emulating them; just as not prizing rare treasures deters a man from becoming a thief; or ignoring the things which awaken desire keeps the heart at rest.

Therefore the wise ruler does not suggest unnecessary things, but seeks to satisfy the minds of his people. He seeks to allay appetites but strengthen bones. He ever tries by keeping people in ignorance to keep them satisfied and those who have knowledge he restrains from evil. If he, himself, practices restraint then everything is in quietness.

4

The Tao appears to be emptiness but it is never exhausted. Oh, it is profound! It appears to have preceded everything. It dulls its own sharpness, unravels its own fetters, softens its own brightness, identifies itself with its own dust.

Oh, it is tranquil! It appears infinite; I do not know from what it proceeds. It even appears to be antecedent to the Lord.

5

Heaven and earth are not like humans, they are impartial. They regard all things as insignificant, as though they were playthings made of straw. The wise man is also impartial. To him all men are alike and unimportant. The space between heaven and earth is like a bellows, it is empty but does not collapse; it moves and more and more issues. A gossip is soon empty, it is doubtful if he can be impartial.

6

The Spirit of the perennial spring is said to be immortal, she is called the Mysterious One. The Mysterious One is typical of the source of heaven and earth. It is continually and endlessly issuing and without effort.

7

Heaven is eternal, earth is lasting. The reason why heaven and earth are eternal and lasting is because they do not live for themselves; that is the reason they will ever endure.

Therefore the wise man will keep his personality out of sight and because of so doing he will become notable. He subordinates his personality and therefore it is preserved.

Is it not because he is disinterested, that his own interests are conserved?

8

True goodness is like water, in that it benefits everything and harms nothing. Like water it ever seeks the lowest place, the place that all others avoid. It is closely kin to the Tao.

For a dwelling it chooses the quiet meadow; for a heart the circling eddy. In generosity it is kind; in speech it is sincere; in authority it is order; in affairs it is ability; in movement it is rhythm.

Inasmuch as it is always peaceable it is never rebuked.

9

Continuing to fill a pail after it is full the water will be wasted. Continuing to grind an axe after it is sharp will soon wear it away.

Who can protect a public hall crowded with gold and jewels? The pride of wealth and position brings about their own misfortune. To win true merit, to preserve just fame, the personality must be retiring. This is the heavenly Tao.

10

What Is Possible

By patience the animal spirits can be disciplined. By self-control one can unify the character. By close attention to the will, compelling gentleness, one can become like a little child. By purifying the subconscious desires one may be without fault. In ruling his country, if the wise magistrate loves his people, he can avoid compulsion.

In measuring out rewards, the wise magistrate will act like a mother bird. While sharply penetrating into every corner, he may appear to be unsuspecting. While quickening and feeding his people, he will be producing but without pride of ownership. He will benefit but without claim of reward. He will persuade, but not compel by force. This is teh, the profoundest virtue.

11

The Value of Non-Existence

Although the wheel has thirty spokes its utility lies in the emptiness of the hub. The jar is made by kneading clay, but its usefulness consists in its capacity. A room is made by cutting out windows and doors through the walls, but the space the walls contain measures the room's value.

In the same way matter is necessary to form, but the value of reality lies in its immateriality.

(Or thus: a material body is necessary to existence, but the value of a life is measured by its immaterial soul.)

12

Avoiding Desire

An excess of light blinds the human eye; an excess of noise ruins the ear; an excess of condiments deadens the taste. The effect of too much horse racing and hunting is bad, and the lure of hidden treasure tempts one to do evil.

Therefore the wise man attends to the inner significance of things and does not concern himself with outward appearances. Therefore he ignores matter and seeks the spirit.

13

Loathing Shame

Favor and disgrace are alike to be feared, just as too great care or anxiety are bad for the body.

Why are favor and disgrace alike to be feared? To be favored is humiliating; to obtain it is as much to be dreaded as to lose it. To lose favor is to be in disgrace and of course is to be dreaded.

Why are excessive care and great anxiety alike bad for one? The very reason I have anxiety is because I have a body. If I have not body why would I be anxious?

Therefore if he who administers the empire, esteems it as his own body, then he is worthy to be trusted with the empire.

14

In Praise of the Profound

It is unseen because it is colorless; it is unheard because it is soundless; when seeking to grasp it, it eludes one, because it is incorporeal.

Because of these qualities it cannot be examined, and yet they form an essential unity. Superficially it appears abstruse, but in its depths it is not obscure. It has been nameless forever! It appears and then disappears. It is what is known as the form of the formless, the image of the imageless. It is called the transcendental, its face (or destiny) cannot be seen in front, or its back (or origin) behind.

But by holding fast to the Tao of the ancients, the wise man may understand the present, because he knows the origin of the past. This is the clue to the Tao.

15

That Which Reveals Teh

In olden times the ones who were considered worthy to be called masters were subtle, spiritual, profound, wise. Their thoughts could not be easily understood.

Since they were hard to understand I will try to make them clear. They were cautious like men wading a river in winter. They were reluctant like men who feared their neighbors. They were reserved like guests in the presence of their host. They were elusive like ice at the point of melting. They were like unseasoned wood. They were like a valley between high mountains. They were obscure like troubled waters. (They were cautious because they were conscious of the deeper meanings of life and its possibilities.)

We can clarify troubled waters by slowly quieting them. We can bring the unconscious to life by slowly moving them. But he who has the secret of the Tao does not desire for more. Being content, he is able to mature without desire to be newly fashioned.

16

Returning to the Source

Seek to attain an open mind (the summit of vacuity). Seek composure (the essence of tranquillity).

All things are in process, rising and returning. Plants come to blossom, but only to return to the root. Returning to the root is like seeking tranquillity; it is moving towards its destiny. To move toward destiny is like eternity. To know eternity is enlightenment, and not to recognize eternity brings disorder and evil.

Knowing eternity makes one comprehensive; comprehension makes one broadminded; breadth of vision brings nobility; nobility is like heaven.

The heavenly is like Tao. Tao is the Eternal. The decay of the body is not to be feared.

17

Simplicity of Habit

When great men rule, subjects know little of their existence. Rulers who are less great win the affection and praise of their subjects. A common ruler is feared by his subjects, and an unworthy ruler is despised.

When a ruler lacks faith, you may seek in vain for it among his subjects.

How carefully a wise ruler chooses his words. He performs deeds, and accumulates merit! Under such a ruler the people think they are ruling themselves.

18

The Palliation of the Inferior

When the great Tao is lost sight of, we still have the idea of benevolence and righteousness. Prudence and wisdom come to mind when we see great hypocrisy. When relatives are! unfriendly, we still have the teachings of filial piety and paternal affection. When the state and the clan are in confusion and disorder, we still have the ideals of loyalty and faithfulness.

19

Return to Simplicity

Abandon the show of saintliness and relinquish excessive prudence, then people will benefit a hundredfold. Abandon ostentatious benevolence and conspicuous righteousness, then people will return to the primal virtues of filial piety and parental affection. Abandon cleverness and relinquish gains, then thieves and robbers will disappear.

Here are three fundamentals on which to depend, wherein culture is insufficient. Therefore let all men hold to that which is reliable, namely, recognize simplicity, cherish purity, reduce one's possessions, diminish one's desires.

20

The Opposite of the Commonplace

Avoid learning if you would have no anxiety. The "yes" and the "yea" differ very little, but the contrast between good and evil is very great. That which is not feared by the people is not worth fearing. But, oh, the difference, the desolation, the vastness, between ignorance and the limitless expression of the Tao.

(The balance of this sonnet is devoted to showing the difference between the careless state of the common people and his own vision of the Tao. It is one of the most pathetic expressions of human loneliness, from lack of appreciation, ever written. It is omitted here that it might serve for the closing sonnet and valedictory.)

21

The Heart of Emptiness

All the innumerable forms of teh correspond to the norm of Tao, but the nature of the Tao's activity is infinitely abstract and illusive. Illusive and obscure, indeed, but at its heart are forms and types. Vague and illusive, indeed, but at its heart is all being. Unfathomable and obscure, indeed, but at its heart is all spirit, and spirit is reality. At its heart is truth.

From of old its expression is unceasing, it has been present at all beginnings. How do I know that its nature is thus? By this same Tao.

22

Increase by Humility

At that time the deficient will be made perfect; the distorted will be straightened; the empty will be filled; the worn out will be renewed; those having little will obtain and those having much will be overcome.

Therefore the wise man, embracing unity as he does, will become the world's model. Not pushing himself forward he will become enlightened; not asserting himself he will become distinguished; not boasting of himself he will acquire merit; not approving himself he will endure. Forasmuch as he will not quarrel, the world will not quarrel with him.

Is the old saying, "The crooked shall be made straight," a false saying? Indeed, no! They will be perfected and return rejoicing.

23

Emptiness and Not-Doing (Wu Wei)

Taciturnity is natural to man. A whirlwind never outlasts the morning, nor a violent rain the day. What is the cause? It is heaven and earth. If even heaven and earth are not constant, much less can man be.

Therefore he who pursues his affairs in the spirit of Tao will become Tao-like. He who pursues his affairs with teh, will become teh-like. He who pursues his affairs with loss, identifies himself with loss.

He who identifies himself with Tao, Tao rejoices to guide. He who identifies himself with teh, teh rejoices to reward. And he who identifies himself with loss, loss rejoices to ruin.

If his faith fail, he will receive no reward of faith.

24

Troubles and Merit

It is not natural to stand on tiptoe, or being astride one does not walk. One who displays himself is not bright, or one who asserts himself cannot shine. A self-approving man has no merit, nor does one who praises himself grow.

The relation of these things (self-display, self-assertion, self-approval) to Tao is the same as offal is to food. They are excrescences from the system; they are detestable; Tao does not dwell in them.

25

Describing the Mysterious

There is Being that is all-inclusive and that existed before Heaven and Earth. Calm, indeed, and incorporeal! It is alone and changeless!

Everywhere it functions unhindered. It thereby becomes the world's mother. I do not know its nature; if I try to characterize it, I will call it Tao.

If forced to give it a name, I will call it the Great. The Great is evasive, the evasive is the distant, the distant is ever coming near. Tao is Great. So is Heaven great, and so is Earth and so also is the representative of Heaven and Earth.

Man is derived from nature, nature is derived from Heaven, Heaven is derived from Tao. Tao is self-derived.

26

The Virtue (Teh) of Dignity

The heavy is the root of the light; the quiet is master of motion. Therefore the wise man in all the experience of the day will not depart from dignity. Though he be surrounded with sights that are magnificent, he will remain calm and unconcerned.

How does it come to pass that the Emperor, master of ten thousand chariots, has lost the mastery of the Empire? Because being flippant himself, he has lost the respect of his subjects; being passionate himself, he has lost the control of the Empire.

27

The Function of Skill

Good walkers leave no tracks, good speakers make no errors, good counters need no abacus, good wardens have no need for bolts and locks for no one can get by them. Good binders can dispense with rope and cord, yet none can unloose their hold.

Therefore the wise man trusting in goodness always saves men, for there is no outcast to him. Trusting in goodness he saves all things for there is nothing valueless to him. This is recognizing concealed values.

Therefore the good man is the instructor of the evil man, and the evil man is the good man's wealth. He who does not esteem his instructors or value his wealth, though he be otherwise intelligent, becomes confused. Herein lies the significance of spirituality.

28

Returning to Simplicity

He who knows his manhood and understands his womanhood becomes useful like the valleys of earth (which bring water). Being like the valleys of earth, eternal vitality (teh) will not depart from him, he will come again to the nature of a little child.

He who knows his innocence and recognizes his sin becomes the world's model. Being a world's model, infinite teh will not fail, he will return to the Absolute.

He who knows the glory of his nature and recognizes also his limitations becomes useful like the world's valleys. Being like the world's valleys, eternal teh will not fail him, he will revert to simplicity.

Radiating simplicity he will make of men vessels of usefulness. The wise man then will employ them as officials and chiefs. A great administration of such will harm no one.

29

Not Forcing Things (Wu Wei)

One who desires to take and remake the Empire will fail. The Empire is a divine thing that cannot be remade. He who attempts it will only mar it.

He who seeks to grasp it, will lose it. People differ, some lead, others follow; some are ardent, others are formal; some are strong, others weak; some succeed, others fail. Therefore the wise man practices moderation; he abandons pleasure, extravagance and indulgence.

30

Be Stingy of War

When the magistrate follows Tao, he has no need to resort to force of arms to strengthen the Empire, because his business methods alone will show good returns.

Briars and thorns grow rank where an army camps. Bad harvests are the sequence of a great war. The good ruler will be resolute and then stop, he dare not take by force. One should be resolute but not boastful; resolute but not haughty; resolute but not arrogant; resolute but yielding when it cannot be avoided; resolute but he must not resort to violence.

By a resort to force, things flourish for a time but then decay. This is not like the Tao and that which is not Tao-like will soon cease.

31

Avoiding War

Even successful arms, among all implements, are unblessed. All men come to detest them. Therefore the one who follows Tao does not rely on them. Arms are of all tools unblessed, they are not the implements of a wise man. Only as a last resort does he use them.

Peace and quietude are esteemed by the wise man, and even when victorious he does not rejoice, because rejoicing over a victory is the same as rejoicing over the killing of men. If he rejoices over killing men, do you think he will ever really master the Empire?

In propitious affairs the place of honor is the left, but in unpropitious affairs we honor the right.

The strong man while at home esteems the left as the place of honor, but when armed for war it is as though he esteems the right hand, the place of less honor.

Thus a funeral ceremony is so arranged. The place of a subordinate army officer is also on the left and the place of his superior officer is on the right. The killing of men fills multitudes with sorrow; we lament with tears because of it, and rightly honor the victor as if he was attending a funeral ceremony.

32

The Virtue (Teh) of Holiness

Tao in its eternal aspect is unnamable. Its simplicity appears insignificant, but the whole world cannot control it. If princes and kings employ it every one of themselves will pay willing homage. Heaven and Earth by it are harmoniously combined and drop sweet dew. People will have no need of rulers, because of themselves they will be righteous.

As soon as Tao expresses itself in orderly creation then it becomes comprehensible. When one recognizes the presence of Tao he understands where to stop. Knowing where to stop he is free from danger.

To illustrate the nature of Tao's place in the universe: Tao is like the brooks and streams in their relation to the great rivers and the ocean.

33

The Virtue (Teh) of Discrimination

He who knows others is intelligent; he who understands himself is enlightened; he who is able to conquer others has force, but he who is able to control himself is mighty. He who appreciates contentment is wealthy.

He who dares to act has nerve; if he can maintain his position he will endure, but he, who dying does not perish, is immortal.

34

The Perfection of Trust

Great Tao is all pervading! It can be on both the right hand and the left. Everything relies upon it for their existence, and it does not fail them. It acquires merit but covets not the title. It lovingly nourishes everything, but does not claim the rights of ownership. It has no desires, it can be classed with the small. Everything returns to it, yet it does not claim the right of ownership. It can be classed with the great.

Therefore the wise man to the end will not pose as a great man, and by so doing will express his true greatness.

35

The Virtue (Teh) of Benevolence

The world will go to him who grasps this Great Principle; they will seek and not be injured, they will find contentment, peace and rest.

Music and dainties attract the passing people, while Tao's reality seen-is insipid. Indeed it has no taste, when looked at there is not enough seen to be prized, when listened for, it can scarcely be heard, but, the use of it is inexhaustible.

36

Explanation of a Paradox

That which has a tendency to contract must first have been extended; that which has a tendency to weaken itself must first have been strong; that which shows a tendency to destroy itself must first have been raised up; that which shows a tendency to scatter must first have been gathered.

This is the explanation of a seeming contradiction: the tender and yielding conquer the rigid and strong (i.e., spirit is stronger than matter, persuasion than force). The fish would be foolish to seek escape from its natural environment. There is no gain to a nation to compel by a show of force.

37

Administering the Government

Tao is apparently inactive (wu wei) and yet nothing remains undone. If princes and kings desire to keep) everything in order, they must first reform themselves. (If princes and kings would follow the example of Tao, then all things will reform themselves.) If they still desire to change, I would pacify them by the simplicity of the ineffable Tao.

This simplicity will end desire, and if desire be absent there is quietness. All people will of themselves be satisfied.

38

A Discussion about Teh

Essential teh makes no show of virtue, and therefore it is really virtuous. Inferior virtue never loses sight of itself and therefore it is no longer virtue. Essential virtue is characterized by lack of self-assertion (wu wei) and therefore is unpretentious. Inferior virtue is acting a part and thereby is only pretense.

Superior benevolence in a way is acting but does not thereby become pretentious. Excessive righteousness is acting and does thereby become pretentious. Excessive propriety is acting, but where no one responds to it, it stretches its arm and enforces obedience.

Therefore when one loses Tao there is still teh; one may lose teh and benevolence remains; one may forsake benevolence and still hold to righteousness; one may lose righteousness and propriety remains.

Propriety, alone, reduces loyalty and good faith to a shadow, and it is the beginning of disorder. Tradition is the mere flower of the Tao and had its origin in ignorance.

Therefore the great man of affairs conforms to the spirit and not to external appearance. He goes on to fruitage and does not rest in the show of blossom. He avoids mere propriety and practices true benevolence.

39

The Root of Authority

It has been said of old, only those who attain unity attain self-hood. . . . Heaven attained unity and thereby is space. Earth attained unity, thereby it is solid. Spirit attained unity, thereby it became mind. Valleys attained unity, therefore rivers flow down them. All things have unity and thereby have life. Princes and kings as they attain unity become standards of conduct for the nation. And the highest unity is that which produces unity.

If heaven were not space it might crack, if earth were not solid it might bend. If spirits were not unified into mind they might vanish, if valleys were not adapted to rivers they would be parched. Everything if it were not for life would burn up. Even princes and kings if they overestimate themselves and cease to be standards will presumably fall.

Therefore nobles find their roots among the commoners; the high is always founded upon the low. The reason why princes and kings speak of themselves as orphans, inferiors and unworthy, is because they recognize that their roots run down to the common life; is it not so?

If a carriage goes to pieces it is no longer a carriage, its unity is gone. A true self-hood does not desire to be overvalued as a gem, nor to be undervalued as a mere stone.

40

Avoiding Activity

Retirement is characteristic of Tao just as weakness appears to be a characteristic of its activity.

Heaven and earth and everything are produced from existence, but existence comes from nonexistence. . . .

41

The Unreality of Appearance

The superior scholar when he considers Tao earnestly practices it; an average scholar listening to Tao sometimes follows it and sometimes loses it; an inferior scholar listening to Tao ridicules it. Were it not thus ridiculed it could not be regarded as Tao.

Therefore the writer says: Those who are most illumined by Tao are the most obscure. Those advanced in Tao are most retiring. Those best guided by Tao are the least prepossessing.

The high in virtue (teh) resemble a lowly valley; the whitest are most likely to be put to shame; the broadest in virtue resemble the inefficient. The most firmly established in virtue resemble the remiss. The simplest chastity resembles the fickle, the greatest square has no corner, the largest vessel is never filled. The greatest sound is void of speech, the greatest form has no shape. Tao is obscure and without name, and yet it is precisely this Tao that alone can give and complete.

42

The Transformation of Tao

Tao produces unity; unity produces duality; duality produces trinity; trinity produces all things. All things bear the negative principle (yin) and embrace the positive principle (yang). Immaterial vitality, the third principle (chi), makes them harmonious.

Those things which are detested by the common people, namely to be called orphans, inferiors, and unworthies, are the very things kings and lords take for titles. There are some things which it is a gain to lose, and a loss to gain.

I am teaching the same things which are taught by others. But the strong and aggressive: ones do not obtain a natural death (i.e., self-confident teachers do not succeed). I alone expound the basis of the doctrine of the Tao.

43

The Function of the Universal

The most tender things of creation race over the hardest.

A non-material existence enters into the most impenetrable.

I therefore recognize an advantage in the doctrine of not doing (wu wei) and not speaking. But there are few in the world who obtain the advantage of non-assertion (wu wei) and silence.

44

Precepts

Which is nearer, a name or a person? Which is more, personality or treasure? Is it more painful to gain or to suffer loss?

Extreme indulgence certainly greatly wastes. Much hoarding certainly invites severe loss.

A contented person is not despised. One who knows when to stop is not endangered; he will be able therefore to continue.

45

The Virtue (Teh) of Greatness

Extreme perfection seems imperfect, its function is not exhausted. Extreme fullness appears empty, its function is not exercised.

Extreme straightness appears crooked; great skill, clumsy; great eloquence, stammering. Motion conquers cold, quietude conquers heat. Not greatness but purity and clearness are the world's standard.

46

Limitation of Desire

When the world yields to Tao, race horses will be used to haul manure. When the world ignores Tao war horses are pastured on the public common.

There is no sin greater than desire. There is no misfortune greater than discontent. There is no calamity greater than acquisitiveness.

Therefore to know extreme contentment is simply to be content.

47

Seeing the Distant

Not going out of the door I have knowledge of the world. Not peeping through the window I perceive heaven's Tao. The more one wanders to a distance the less he knows.

Therefore the wise man does not wander about but he understands, he does not see things but he defines them, he does not labor yet he completes.

48

To Forget Knowledge

He who attends daily to learning increases in learning. He who practices Tao daily diminishes. Again and again he humbles himself. Thus he attains to non-doing (wu wei). He practices non-doing and yet there is nothing left undone.

To command the empire one must not employ craft. If one uses craft he is not fit to command the empire.

49

The Virtue (Teh) of Trust

The wise man has no fixed heart; in the hearts of the people he finds his own. The good he treats with goodness; the not-good he also treats with goodness, for teh is goodness. The faithful ones he treats with good faith; the unfaithful he also treats with good faith, for teh is good faith.

The wise man lives in the world but he lives cautiously, dealing with the world cautiously. He universalizes his heart; the people give him their eyes and ears, but he treats them as his children.

50

Esteem Life

Life is a going forth; death is a returning home. Of ten, three are seeking life, three are seeking death, and three are dying. What is the reason? Because they live in life's experience. (Only one is immortal.)

I hear it said that the sage when he travels is never attacked by rhinoceros or tiger, and when coming among soldiers does not fear their weapons. The rhinoceros would find no place to horn him, nor the tiger a place for his claws, nor could soldiers wound him. What is the reason? Because he is invulnerable.

51

Teh as a Nurse

Tao gives life to all creatures; teh feeds them; materiality shapes them; energy completes them. Therefore among all things there is none that does not honor Tao and esteem teh. Honor for Tao and esteem for teh is never compelled, it is always spontaneous. Therefore Tao gives life to them, but teh nurses them, raises them, nurtures, completes, matures, rears, protects them.

Tao gives life to them but makes no claim of ownership; teh forms them but makes no claim upon them, raises them but does not rule them. This is profound vitality (teh).

52

Return to Origin

When creation began, Tao became the world's mother. When one knows one's mother he will m turn know that he is her son. When he recognizes his sonship, he will in turn keep to his mother and to the end of life will be free from danger.

He who closes his mouth and shuts his sense gates will be free from trouble to the end of life. He who opens his mouth and meddles with affairs cannot be free from trouble even to the end of life.

To recognize one's insignificance is called enlightenment. To keep one's sympathy is called strength. He who uses Tao's light returns to Tao's enlightenment and does not surrender his person to perdition. This is called practicing the eternal.

53

Gain by Insight

Even if one has but a little knowledge he can walk in the ways of the great Tao; it is only self-assertion that one need fear.

The great Tao (Way) is very plain, but people prefer the bypaths. When the palace is very splendid, the fields are likely to be very weedy, and the granaries empty. To wear ornaments and gay colors, to carry sharp swords, to be excessive in eating and drinking, and to have wealth and treasure in abundance is to know the pride of robbers. This is contrary to Tao.

54

To Cultivate Intuition

The thing that is well planted is not easily uprooted. The thing that is well guarded is not easily taken away. If one has sons and grandsons, the offering of ancestral worship will not soon cease.

He who practices Tao in his person shows that his teh is real. The family that practices it shows that their teh is abounding. The township that practices it shows that their teh is enduring. The state that practices it shows that their teh is prolific. The empire that practices it reveals that teh is universal. Thereby one person becomes a test of other persons, one family of other families, one town of other towns, one county of other counties, and one empire of all empires.

How do I know that this test is universal? By this same Tao.

55

to Verify the Mysterious

The essence of teh is comparable to the state of a young boy. Poisonous insects will not sting him, wild beasts will not seize him, birds of prey will not attack him. The bones are weak, the muscles are tender, it is true, but his grasp is firm.

He does not yet know the relation of the sexes, but he has perfect organs, nevertheless. His spirit is virile, indeed! He can sob and cry all day without becoming hoarse, his harmony (as a child) is perfect indeed!

To recognize this harmony (for growth) is to know the eternal'. To recognize the eternal is to know enlightenment. To increase life (to cause things to grow) is to know blessedness. To be conscious of an inner fecundity is strength. Things fully grown are about to decay, they are the opposite of Tao. The opposite of Tao soon ceases.

56

The Teh of the Mysterious

The one who knows does not speak; the one who speaks does not know. The wise man shuts his mouth and closes his gates. He softens his sharpness, unravels his tangles, dims his brilliancy, and reckons himself with the mysterious.

He is inaccessible to favor or hate; he cannot be reached by profit or injury; he cannot be honored or humiliated. Thereby he is honored by all.

57

The Habit of Simplicity

The empire is administered with righteousness; the army is directed by craft; the people are captivated by non-diplomacy. How do I know it is so? By this same Tao.

Among people the more restrictions and prohibitions there are, the poorer they become. The more people have weapons, the more the state is in confusion. The more people are artful and cunning the more abnormal things occur. The more laws and orders are issued the more thieves and robbers abound.

Therefore the wise man says: If a ruler practices wu wei the people will reform of themselves. If I love quietude the people will of themselves become righteous. If I avoid profit-making the people will of themselves become prosperous. If I limit my desires the people will of themselves become simple.

58

Adaptation to Change

When an administration is unostentatious the people are simple. When an administration is inquisitive, the people are needy. Misery, alas, supports happiness. Happiness, alas, conceals misery. Who knows its limits? It never ceases. The normal becomes the abnormal. The good in turn becomes unlucky. The people's confusion is felt daily for a long time.

Therefore the wise man is square, yet does not injure, he is angular but does not annoy. He is upright but is not cross. He is bright but not glaring.

59

To Keep Tao

In governing the people and in worshipping heaven nothing surpasses moderation. To value moderation, one must form the habit early. Its early acquisition will result in storing and accumulating vitality. By storing and accumulating vitality nothing is impossible.

If nothing is impossible then one is ignorant of his limits. If one does not know his limitations, one may possess the state. He who possesses moderation is thereby lasting and enduring. It is like having deep roots and a strong stem. This is of long life and enduring insight the Tao (way).

60

To Maintain Position

One should govern a great state as one fries small fish (i.e., do not scale or clean them).

With Tao one may successfully rule the Empire. Ghosts will not frighten, gods will not harm, neither will wise men mislead the people. Since nothing frightens or harms the people, teh will abide.

61

The Teh of Humility

A great state that is useful is like a bond of unity within the Empire; it is the Empire's wife.

The female controls the male by her quietude and submission. Thus a great state by its service to smaller states wins their allegiance. A small state by submission to a great state wins an influence over them. Thus some stoop to conquer, and others stoop and conquer.

Great states can have no higher purpose than to federate states and feed the people. Small states can have no higher purpose than to enter a federation and serve the people. Both alike, each in his own way, gain their end, but to do so, the greater must practice humility.

62

The Practice of Tao

The Tao is the asylum of all things; the good man's treasure, the bad man's last resort. With beautiful words one may sell goods but in winning people one can accomplish more by kindness. Why should a man be thrown away for his evil? To conserve him was the Emperor appointed and the three ministers.

Better than being in the presence of the Emperor and riding with four horses, is sitting and explaining this Tao.

The reason the Ancients esteemed Tao was because if sought it was obtained, and because by it he that hath sin could be saved. Is it not so? Therefore the world honors Tao.

63

A Consideration of Beginnings

One should avoid assertion (wu wei) and practice inaction. One should learn to find taste in the tasteless, to enlarge the small things, and multiply the few. He should respond to hatred with kindness. He should resolve a difficulty while it is easy, and manage a great thing while it is small. Surely all the world's difficulties arose from slight causes, and all the world's great affairs had small beginnings.

Therefore the wise man avoids to the end participation in great affairs and by so doing establishes his greatness.

Rash promises are lacking in faith and many things that appear easy are full of difficulties. Therefore the wise man considers every thing difficult and so to the end he has no difficulties.

64

Consider the Insignificant

That which is at rest is easily restrained, that which has not yet appeared is easily prevented. The weak is easily broken, the scanty is easily scattered. Consider a difficulty before it arises, and administer affairs before they become disorganized. A tree that it takes both arms to encircle grew from a tiny rootlet. A pagoda of nine stories was erected by placing small bricks. A journey of three thousand miles begins with one step. If one tries to improve a thing, he mars it; if he seizes it, he loses it. The wise man, therefore, not attempting to form things does not mar them, and not grasping after things he does not lose them. The people in their rush for business are ever approaching success but continually failing. One must be as careful to the end as at the beginning if he is to succeed.

Therefore the wise man desires to be free from desire, he does not value the things that are difficult of attainment. He learns to be unlearned, he returns to that which all others ignore. In that spirit he helps all things toward their natural development, but dares not interfere.

65

The Teh of Simplicity

In the olden days those who obeyed the spirit of Tao did not enlighten the people but kept them simple hearted.

The reason people are difficult to govern is because of their smartness; likewise to govern a people with guile is a curse; and to govern them with simplicity is a blessing. He who remembers these two things is a model ruler. Always to follow this standard and rule is teh, the profound.

Profound teh is deep indeed and far reaching. The very opposite of common things, but by it one obtains obedient subjects.

66

To Subordinate Self

The reason rivers and seas are called the kings of the valley is because they keep below them.

Therefore the wise man desiring to be above his people must in his demeanor keep below them; wishing to benefit his people, he must ever keep himself out of sight.

The wise man dwells above, yet the people do not feel the burden; he is the leader and the people suffer no harm. Therefore the world rejoices to exalt him and never wearies of him.

Because he will not quarrel with anyone, no one can quarrel with him.

67

Three Treasures

All the world calls Tao great, yet it is by nature immaterial. It is because a thing is seemingly unreal that it is great. If a man affects to be great, how long can he conceal his mediocrity?

Tao has three treasures which he guards and cherishes. The first is called compassion; the second is called economy; the third is called humility. A man that is compassionate can 'be truly brave; if a man is economical he can be generous; if he is humble he can become a useful servant.

If one discards compassion and is still brave, abandons economy and is still generous, forsakes humility and still seeks to be serviceable, his days are numbered. On the contrary if one is truly compassionate, in battle he will be a conqueror and in defence he will be secure. When even Heaven helps people it is because of compassion that she does so.

68

Compliance with Heaven

He who excels as a soldier is the one who is not warlike; he who fights the best fight is not wrathful; he who best conquers an enemy is not quarrelsome; he who best employs people is obedient himself.

This is the virtue of not-quarreling, this is the secret of bringing out other men's ability, this is complying with Heaven. Since of old it is considered the greatest virtue (teh).

69

The Function of the Mysterious

A military expert has said: I do not dare put myself forward as a host, but always act as a guest. I hesitate to advance an inch, but am willing to withdraw a foot.

This is advancing by not advancing, it is winning without arms, it is charging without hostility, it is seizing without weapons. There is no mistake greater than making light of an enemy. By making light of an enemy we lose our treasure.

Therefore when well-matched armies come to conflict, the one who is conscious of his weakness conquers.

70

The Difficulty of Understanding

My words are very easy to understand and very easy to put into practice, yet in all the world no one appears to understand them or to practice them.

Words have an ancestor (a preceding idea), deeds have a master (a preceding purpose), and just as these are often not understood, so I am not understood.

They who understand me are very few, and on that account I am worthy of honor. The wise man wears wool (rather than silk) and keeps his gems out of sight.

71

The Disease of Knowledge

To recognize one's ignorance of unknowable things is mental health, and to be ignorant of knowable things is sickness. Only by grieving over ignorance of knowable things are we in mental health. The wise man is wise because he understands his ignorance and is grieved over it.

72

To Cherish One's Self

When people are too ignorant to fear the fearsome thing, then it will surely come. Do not make the place where they dwell confining, the life they live wearisome. If they are let alone, they will not become restless. Therefore the wise man while not understanding himself regards himself, while cherishing he does not overvalue himself. Therefore he discards flattery and prefers regard.

73

Action Is Dangerous

Courage carried to daring leads to death. Courage restrained by caution leads to life. These two things, courage and caution, are sometimes beneficial and sometimes harmful. Some things are rejected by heaven, who can tell the reason? Therefore the wise man deems all acting difficult.

The Tao of heaven does not quarrel, yet it conquers. It speaks not, yet its response is good. It issues no summons but things come to it naturally because its devices are good. Heaven's net is vast, indeed! its meshes are wide but it loses nothing.

74

Overcoming Delusions

If the people do not fear death, how can one frighten them with death? If we teach people to fear death, then when one rebels he can be seized and executed; after that who will dare to rebel?

There is always an officer to execute a murderer, but if one takes the place of the executioner, it is like taking the place of a skilled carpenter at his hewing. If one takes the place of the skilled carpenter he is liable to cut himself. (Therefore do not interfere with Tao.)

75

Loss by Greediness

Starvation of a people comes when an official appropriates to himself too much of the taxes. The reason a people are difficult to govern is because the officials are too meddlesome; the people make light of death because they are so absorbed in life's interests. The one who is not absorbed in life is more moral than he who esteems life.

76

Beware of Strength

When a man is living he is tender and fragile. When he dies he is hard and stiff. It is the same with everything, the grass and trees, in life, are tender and delicate, but when they die they become rigid and dry.

Therefore those who are hard and stiff belong to death's domain, while the tender and weak belong to the realm of life.

Therefore soldiers are most invincible when they will not conquer. When a tree is grown to its greatest strength it is doomed. The strong and the great stay below; the tender and weak rise above.

77

Tao of Heaven

Tao of heaven resembles the stretching of a bow. The mighty it humbles, the lowly it exalts. They who have abundance it diminishes and gives to them who have need.

That is Tao of heaven; it depletes those who abound, and completes those who lack.

The human way is not so. Men take from those who lack to give to those who already abound. Where is the man who by his abundance can best serve the world?

The wise man makes but claims not, he accomplishes merit, yet is not attached to it, neither does he display his excellence. Is it not so?

78

Trust and Faith

In the world nothing is more fragile than water, and yet of all the agencies that attack hard substances nothing can surpass it.

Of all things there is nothing that can take the place of Tao. By it the weak are conquerors of the strong, the pliable are conquerors of the rigid. In the world every one knows this, but none practice it.

Therefore the wise man declares: he who is guilty of the country's sin may be the priest at the altar. He who is to blame for the country's misfortunes, is often the Empire's Sovereign. True words are often paradoxical.

79

Enforcing Contracts

When reconciling great hatred there will some remain. How can it be made good?

Therefore the wise man accepts the debit side of the account and does not have to enforce payment from others. They who have virtue (teh) keep their obligations, they who have no virtue insist on their rights. Tao of heaven has no favorites but always helps the good man.

80

Contentment

In a small country with few people let there be officers over tens and hundreds but not to exercise power. Let the people be not afraid of death, nor desire to move to a distance. Then though there be ships and carriages, they will have no occasion to use them. Though there be armor and weapons there will be no occasion for donning them. The people can return to p. 52 knotted cords for their records, they can delight in their food, be proud of their clothes, be content with their dwellings, rejoice in their customs.

Other states may be close neighbors, their cocks and dogs may be mutually heard, people will come to old age and die but will have no desire to go or come.

81

The Nature of the Essential

Faithful words are often not pleasant; pleasant words are often not faithful. Good men do not dispute; the ones who dispute are not good. The learned men are often not the wise men, nor the wise men, the learned. The wise man does not hoard, but ever working for others, he will the more exceedingly acquire. Having given to others freely, he himself will have in plenty. Tao of heaven benefits but does not injure. The wise man's Tao leads him to act but not to quarrel.

www.ingramcontent.com/pod-product-compliance
Lightning Source LLC
Chambersburg PA
CBHW031414040426
42444CB00005B/555